W9-BNB-527

Other Books by Jeff Kinney

Diary of a Wimpy Kid
Diary of a Wimpy Kid: Rodrick Rules
Diary of a Wimpy Kid: The Last Straw
Diary of a Wimpy Kid: Dog Days
Diary of a Wimpy Kid: The Ugly Truth
Diary of a Wimpy Kid: Cabin Fever
Diary of a Wimpy Kid: The Third Wheel
Diary of a Wimpy Kid: Hard Luck
Diary of a Wimpy Kid: The Long Haul
Diary of a Wimpy Kid: Old School
Diary of a Wimpy Kid: Double Down

DIARY
of a
Wimpy Kid

THE THIRD WHEEL

BY JEFF KINNEY

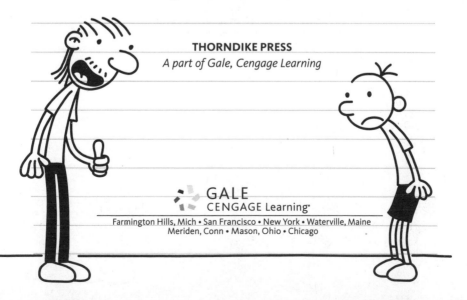

THORNDIKE PRESS
A part of Gale, Cengage Learning

GALE
CENGAGE Learning·

Farmington Hills, Mich • San Francisco • New York • Waterville, Maine
Meriden, Conn • Mason, Ohio • Chicago

GALE
CENGAGE Learning

Thorndike Press® Large Print Mini-Collections.
The text of this Large Print edition is unabridged.
Other aspects of the book may vary from the original edition.
Set in 16 pt. Plantin.

LIBRARY OF CONGRESS CATALOGING-IN-PUBLICATION DATA

Names: Kinney, Jeff, author, illustrator.
Title: Diary of a wimpy kid : the third wheel / by Jeff Kinney.
Other titles: Third wheel
Description: Large print edition. | Waterville, Maine : Thorndike Press,
    2017. | "Thorndike Press Large Print Mini-Collections"—Copyright page. |
    Originally published in a slightly different form by Amulet Books in 2012.
    | Summary: A Valentine's Day dance at Greg's middle school has turned his
    world upside down until an unexpected twist gives Greg a partner for the
    dance and leaves his best friend Rowley the odd man out.
Identifiers: LCCN 2016053576| ISBN 9781410498724 (hardback) | ISBN
    1410498727 (hardcover)
Subjects: LCSH: Large type books. | CYAC: Middle schools—Fiction. |
    Schools—Fiction. | Valentine's Day—Fiction. | Dance parties—Fiction. |
    Best friends—Fiction. | Friendship—Fiction. | Family life—Fiction. |
    Diaries—Fiction. | Humorous stories. | Large type books. | BISAC:
    JUVENILE FICTION / Family / Siblings. | JUVENILE FICTION / Humorous
    Stories.
Classification: LCC PZ7.K6232 Dn 2017 | DDC [Fic]—dc23
LC record available at https://lccn.loc.gov/2016053576

Published in 2017 by arrangement with Amulet Books, an imprint of
Harry N. Abrams, Inc.

Printed in the United States of America
1 2 3 4 5 6 7 21 20 19 18 17

TO GRAM

<u>Sunday</u>

I wish I'd started keeping a journal a lot earlier on, because whoever ends up writing my biography is gonna have a lot of questions about my life in the years leading up to middle school.

Luckily, I remember just about everything that's happened to me since I was born. In fact, I can even remember stuff that happened to me BEFORE I was born.

Back in those days it was just me swimming around in the dark, doing backflips and taking naps whenever I wanted.

Then one day when I was in the middle of a really good nap, I got woken up by these strange noises coming from the outside.

At the time I didn't know what the heck I was hearing, but later on I found out it was Mom piping in music through these speakers she put on her belly.

I guess Mom thought if she played classical music for me every day before I was born, it would turn me into some kind of genius.

Those speakers came with a microphone, and when Mom wasn't playing music, she was telling me everything that was going on in her life.

And when Dad came home from work, Mom would have him give me a blow-by-blow of HIS day.

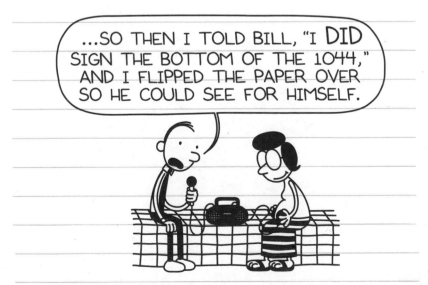

But that wasn't the end of it. Every night, Mom would read to me for a half hour before she went to bed.

The problem is, my sleep schedule didn't line up with Mom's. So when she was sleeping, I'd be wide awake.

I actually wish I'd paid more attention when Mom was reading to me, though.

10

Last week in school we had a pop quiz on a book, and I hadn't read it yet. I was pretty sure Mom read that one to me before I was born, but I couldn't remember any of the details.

I guess the week Mom was reading that book, I was busy doing something else.

The crazy thing is, Mom didn't NEED to use the microphone for me to hear her.

I mean, I was INSIDE of her, so I could hear every word she said whether I wanted to or not.

I could also hear just about EVERYTHING that was happening on the outside. So when Mom and Dad got all mushy, I had to listen to THAT, too.

I've never really felt comfortable when people are acting affectionate around me, ESPECIALLY when it's my parents. I tried to get them to stop, but they never got the message.

In fact, everything I tried just seemed to make things WORSE.

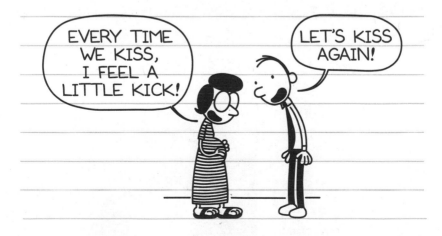

After a few months of living like this, I had to get out of there, and that's why I was born three weeks early. But after being hit by the cold air and the blinding lights of the delivery room, I wished I'd just stayed put.

By the time I came into the world, I was totally sleep deprived and in a really lousy mood. So if you ever see a picture of a newborn, now you know why they always look ticked off.

In fact, I STILL haven't caught up on the sleep I missed, and believe me, I've been trying.

Ever since I was born, I've tried to re-create the feeling I had way back when I was floating around in the dark, happy as could be.

But when you're living in a house with four other people, some fool is always gonna come along and ruin things for you.

I met my older brother, Rodrick, a few days after I was born. Up to that point I thought I was an only child, so I was pretty disappointed to find out I wasn't.

My family was living in a really small apartment back then, and I had to share a room with Rodrick. He got the crib, so for the first few months of my life I had to sleep in the top dresser drawer, which I'm pretty sure isn't even legal.

Eventually, Dad moved his work stuff out of the room he was using as an office and made it into a nursery. I got Rodrick's old crib, and he got a new bed.

Almost EVERYTHING I had back in those days was a hand-me-down from Rodrick.

By the time something came to me, it was either worn-out or covered in slobber.

Even my PACIFIER was a hand-me-down from Rodrick. I don't think he was ready to give it up, though, which might explain why he's never really liked me.

It was just the four of us for a long time, and then one day Mom told me she was gonna have another baby. I was glad she gave me the heads-up so I could be ready.

When my little brother, Manny, came along, everybody thought he was so cute. But what they don't tell you about babies is that after they're born, they have this black stub on their belly button where the umbilical cord was tied off.

Eventually, the stub dries up and falls off, and the baby has a regular-looking belly button. The thing is, nobody ever FOUND Manny's stub. And to this day I'm still paranoid it's gonna show up somewhere.

When I was a newborn, Mom put me in front of the TV for an hour a day to watch educational videos.

I don't know if those videos actually made me any smarter, but at least I was smart enough to figure out how to put on something I WANTED to watch.

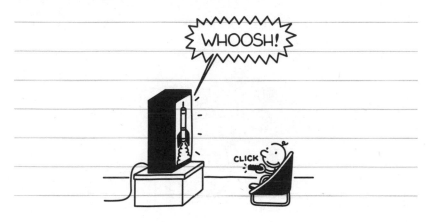

I ALSO figured out how to remove the batteries from the remote so no one could turn the educational videos back ON.

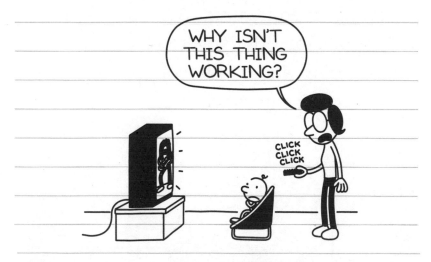

But when you're a baby, you can't really get around a lot, so there was only one place I could hide the batteries.

I think Mom should've let me crawl around on the floor more when I was little, because I was WAY behind the other kids in my playgroup when it came to the physical stuff. While the others were sitting up and couch surfing, I was still working on lifting my head off the ground.

Then one day Mom bought me this thing called a "Baby Adventures Action Walker," which was the first thing I ever got that Rodrick didn't have before me.

The Action Walker was AWESOME. It had a million little gadgets you could entertain yourself with, plus a cup holder.

But the best thing about it was I could get anywhere I needed to go without actually having to WALK.

I could tell that when I was in my Baby Adventures Action Walker, all my little playgroup friends felt like chumps.

But then Mom read in some parenting magazine that it wasn't a good idea to use baby walkers, because kids wouldn't develop the right muscles to walk on their own. So Mom returned the Action Walker to the store, and I was back to square one.

It took a long time, but eventually I DID learn to walk. And before I knew it, I was in preschool.

I was hoping I'd have a head start over the other kids because of all the work Mom had put in with the classical music and the educational DVDs, but the other moms must've done that stuff, too, because the competition in preschool was pretty stiff.

I mean, you had kids in there who knew how to use buttons and zippers, when I could barely figure out how to pull off my mittens without help from a grown-up.

A few of my classmates could write their own names, and one or two could count all the way to fifty.

I knew I couldn't keep up, so I decided to try and slow everyone else down by feeding them bad information.

My plan kind of backfired, though, and my preschool teacher told Mom I wasn't learning my colors and shapes like the other kids. But Mom said I was smart and that maybe the problem was I wasn't being CHALLENGED enough.

So Mom actually took me out of preschool and had me SKIP a grade, to kindergarten. But that decision was a total disaster.

The kids in kindergarten seemed like GIANTS to me, and they knew how to do stuff like cut with scissors and color inside the lines.

I didn't even make it a whole day in kindergarten before the teacher had to call Mom to come get me.

The next day Mom brought me back to preschool and asked the teacher if I could have my cubby back. I just hope your academic record doesn't follow you around, because it might be tough for me to get a good job later on if people find out I was a kindergarten dropout.

<u>Monday</u>

I'm pretty sure Mom decided that whatever she tried with me when I was little didn't work out, because she's taking a totally different approach with Manny.

For starters, Mom pretty much lets Manny watch whatever he wants on TV. So he keeps it on this show called "The Snurples" twenty-four hours a day.

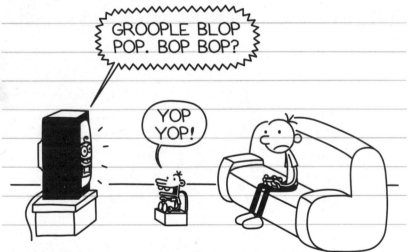

I tried to watch "The Snurples" a few times, but I had NO idea what was going on. The Snurples have their own language that I guess only three-year-olds can understand.

After Manny watches the show, he gets frustrated when no one in our family can understand him.

But the other day Mom read an article in the newspaper that said watching "The Snurples" actually sets kids back about a year with their language development and messes up their social skills, too.

Well, that explains a lot. Manny doesn't have any real friends, and whenever Mom holds playgroup at our house, Manny is the only one who doesn't interact with the other kids.

I think part of the issue is that Manny doesn't like to share his toys. So when kids come over, Manny locks himself inside our old dog Sweetie's exercise pen and keeps his toys all to himself.

And whenever Mom tries to get Manny to play with other kids on his OWN, it backfires.

At our church they have this new thing
where they send all the little kids down to
the basement during the service so they
can play and color. But the first time Mom
dropped Manny off downstairs, there was
only one other kid in the play area, and he
told Manny he was a vampire.

I felt a little bad for Manny because I had
to deal with a scary kid when I was his age,
too. I was stuck in preschool with this boy
named Bradley who terrorized me every
chance he got.

I told Mom about Bradley every day when I came home, and said I didn't want to go to school anymore. But that summer Bradley and his family moved away, so the problem took care of itself.

After Bradley moved, Mom wrote a story called "Bad Bradley," about a kid who always misbehaves. Bradley was a bad kid in real life, but in Mom's version he was pretty much the devil.

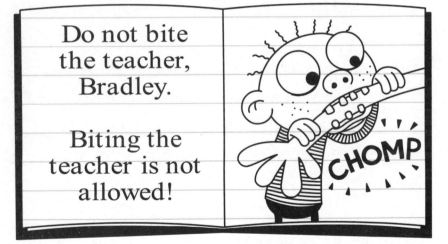

I think Mom was actually gonna try and get her story published, but Bradley and his family moved BACK into our neighborhood the next spring, so she had to scrap it.

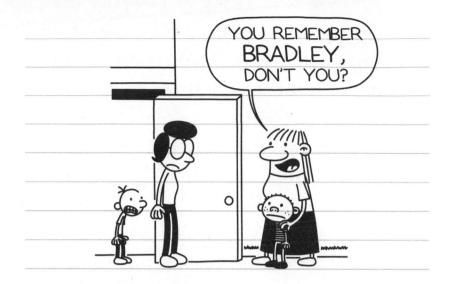

Even though Mom never got her Bad Bradley story published, she used it to teach Manny about how you're supposed to behave in preschool. And I think that's one of the reasons Manny is so afraid of other kids his age.

Manny may not have any REAL friends, but he has a bunch of IMAGINARY ones. I've kind of lost count of them all, but the names I can remember are Joey, Petey, Danny, Charles Tribble, The Other Charles Tribble, Tiny Jim, and Johnny Cheddar.

I don't know how Manny came up with all those fake friends, but believe me, to him they're REAL. One time Manny took all his imaginary friends to the grocery store and had a total meltdown when Mom supposedly left Charles Tribble behind in the frozen foods aisle.

Sometimes I wonder if Manny made up his imaginary friends so he could get stuff like extra dessert after dinner.

Mom says if we tell Manny his so-called friends aren't real, he could be "traumatized." So we just have to go along with it.

I just hope he grows out of this soon, because it's getting kind of ridiculous. Sometimes I have to wait until all of Manny's imaginary friends are done using the bathroom before I can get in.

Lately, Manny has been blaming things he does on his imaginary friends. The other day he smashed a plate on the floor and then told Mom it was Johnny Cheddar, who seems to be the troublemaker of the pack.

Instead of punishing Manny for breaking a plate and then lying about it, Mom gave a time-out to Johnny Cheddar. What really stinks is that the time-out chair is the brand-new recliner in the family room, so I couldn't sit in it to watch television.

Like I said, I know this whole imaginary friend thing is a bunch of baloney, but Manny acts so serious about it that it's kind of spooky. Whenever I go to sit down somewhere in the house, I make sure none of Manny's friends are around.

The last thing I need to do is plop down on the sofa to watch TV and squish Tiny Jim.

It's not like I'm watching a lot of television these days anyway. Mom is pretty worried about Manny and his social skills, so she doesn't like the TV to be on when Manny's around.

Recently, Mom came up with this idea called "Family Night," where we play a board game or go out to dinner together instead of watching TV.

I guess the idea is to get us to interact with one another more so it rubs off on Manny.

When we go out to dinner, we usually end up at this place called Corny's Family-Style Restaurant. They have a rule at Corny's that you're not allowed to wear a tie, and the first time we went there, Dad found that out the hard way.

There are a few different seating sections at Corny's, but since we always have Manny with us, they put our family in the section called "Children's Alley."

In Children's Alley, I don't think they even
bother cleaning up when one family leaves
and a new one comes in. So when you get
to your table, there's always crumpled-up
napkins on the floor and half-eaten french
fries on the seats.

The first time we went to Corny's, I didn't
check my seat, and I ended up sitting on
an open-faced peanut butter and jelly
sandwich.

Another thing I hate about Children's Alley is that you're right next to the bathrooms, and the doors are always swinging open, so you can see in there when you're trying to eat.

Also, the service is TERRIBLE at Corny's, so we always just get the buffet and serve ourselves. The food is in these metal trays, and there's always stuff from one tray mixed in with the others.

At the dessert bar, they have an ice-cream dispenser where you can make your own sundae. I know that sounds great, but there's a reason most restaurants don't let customers operate the soft-serve machines.

One of the reasons Mom likes to go to Corny's is that they have a ball pit, and she's hoping Manny will learn to play with other kids his age.

But Manny usually just buries himself in a
pile of balls to hide from the other kids and
then waits it out until it's time to go home.

Last Thursday we went to Corny's, and
Mom actually made Manny go in the
plastic tubes so he couldn't hide in the
ball pit. Manny got freaked out up there,
though, and he was too scared to come
down on his own.

So Mom told me I had to go up there and get him since I was the only one in the family who was small enough to crawl in the tubes.

I tried climbing up through the area Manny had used to get to the tubes, but it was too tight of a squeeze and I had to bail out.

That meant the only way I could get to Manny was to climb up the spiral plastic slide that empties into the ball pit. I am not a fan of dark, enclosed spaces to begin with, so I wasn't looking forward to crawling up that thing.

I yelled into the bottom to make sure the coast was clear, but kids ignored me and came sliding down anyway.

Once I made it past the traffic jam and got all the way to the top, I started crawling around through the maze of tubes to try and find Manny. There was no ventilation up there, and it REEKED of dirty socks.

I realized I was the wrong person to go looking for Manny, though, because I've always been bad at mazes. This fall me and Mom went in the corn maze at Reynold's Farm, and Mom was counting on me to find the way out.

But I got us so lost that Mom had to call 911 for someone to come rescue us.

This time I didn't have Mom's cell phone to bail me out. And when some kid threw up at one end of the tunnel, all the other kids came rushing my way to get to the slide.

Eventually, I found Manny in one of the tunnels, but by then I was ready to crack up. So one of the waiters had to climb up and rescue Manny AND me.

The worst part of the whole experience was that I had to throw out my favorite pair of jeans because I couldn't get rid of the smell of feet, even after washing them with bleach three times.

Saturday

I woke up at 6:30 this morning and couldn't get back to sleep, which was pretty frustrating. But that's been happening to me ever since the beginning of the year.

46

On New Year's Eve, Mom wanted Manny to feel what it's like to be up at midnight without actually letting him stay up that late. So she set the clocks in the house ahead by three hours.

She didn't tell ME, though. So when Mom and Dad did the countdown with Manny, I thought it was midnight for REAL.

I ended up going to bed at 10:30 that night thinking it was 1:30 in the morning. So my whole schedule has been off by three hours this year.

I don't usually wake up on weekends until Dad literally drags me out of bed, ESPECIALLY during the winter, when it's cold outside and it's nice and warm under the covers.

I remember a time last winter when Dad woke me at 8:00 on a Saturday morning and told me to go outside and shovel snow off the walkway.

I'd been in the middle of a really good dream, but I was able to get out of bed, shovel the walkway, and get right back into my dream without missing a beat.

48

This morning after I woke up, I lay in bed for a while trying to get back to sleep. Eventually, I just went downstairs and made myself some breakfast. There's nothing good on TV before 8:00 on a Saturday morning, so I decided to get some of my chores over with.

Me and Rodrick never have enough money to buy anything, so Mom has been paying us an allowance to do chores. One of my chores is dusting the dining room furniture, and that's what I was doing this morning when I heard a knock at the front door.

I opened the door and was surprised to see Uncle Gary standing on the front steps.

50

Dad came downstairs a minute later, and he didn't seem too happy to see his younger brother.

A few weeks back Uncle Gary called Dad and said he had a "once-in-a-lifetime" business opportunity and needed a loan.

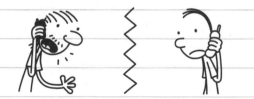

Dad didn't want to give Uncle Gary any money, because Uncle Gary has a bad track record when it comes to paying people back.

But Mom told Dad he should do it because
Uncle Gary is his brother and family
members should always help each other
out. Mom's always saying the same sort
of thing to me and Rodrick. I just hope I
never need a kidney or something like that,
because if Rodrick is the guy I'm counting
on to give it to me, I could be in trouble.

Dad sent Uncle Gary the money, and we
hadn't heard from him until today. After
Uncle Gary came inside the house, he told
us what happened.

He said he met a guy in Boston who sold
T-shirts on a street corner, and this guy
told him that if he wanted to take over his
business, he could make a bundle.

So after he got the money from Dad, Uncle Gary bought up the guy's T-shirts. But what Uncle Gary didn't know was that the T-shirts had a typo on them, and by the time he noticed the problem, the guy was already gone.

Uncle Gary told Dad he needs a place to stay until he can get on his feet again. Dad didn't seem too happy about that, but by then Mom was downstairs, and she told Uncle Gary he can stay as long as he needs.

But when Mom saw the moving van in the driveway, she told Uncle Gary we didn't really have any room in our house for extra furniture.

He said she didn't need to worry, because he didn't HAVE any furniture. The moving van was filled with boxes of T-shirts, which we spent the rest of the morning loading into our garage.

I don't think Uncle Gary is giving up on selling them, either. He unloaded one on Rodrick for three bucks, and I think Rodrick feels like he got a steal.

Monday

Living with Uncle Gary hasn't been easy.
On his first few nights in the house, he slept
on an air mattress in Manny's room. But
Uncle Gary has these nightmares that wake
him up in the middle of the night, and last
Monday he had a really bad one.

THERE'S MONKEYS
IN THE WALLS!
THERE'S MONKEYS
IN THE WALLS!

So now Uncle Gary is sleeping on the couch in the family room, and Manny's bed is in the middle of his room, away from the walls.

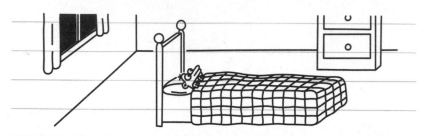

It's really inconvenient with Uncle Gary sleeping on our couch. His bad dreams keep him up all night, and then he sleeps through most of the day. That really stinks when you just want to relax after school and watch some TV.

The person who's been affected the most by Uncle Gary is RODRICK, though.

Before Uncle Gary moved in, Rodrick practically LIVED on the couch in the family room, especially on the weekends.

Now Rodrick doesn't have anywhere to go when Dad kicks him out of bed in the basement on Saturday mornings.

The other day Rodrick came upstairs, and when he saw Uncle Gary in his spot, he just slept on another part of the couch.

Dad has really been nagging Uncle Gary about finding a job, but Uncle Gary says he's tried and no one is hiring.

Uncle Gary has never held down a job for more than a few days. The last one he had was over the summer, when he worked as a test subject for a company that made pepper spray. I'm pretty sure he quit before lunch.

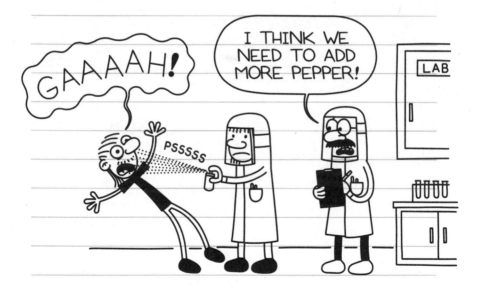

Dad wants Uncle Gary to get a job like HE has, where you work in an office and have regular hours.

But I don't think Uncle Gary is cut out
for an office job, and I'm not so sure I am,
either. Dad has to dress up for work every
day in a shirt and tie, and he has to wear
dress shoes and dress socks, too.

I've already decided that when I grow up,
I'm gonna have to find a job where you
don't need to wear those socks that go up
to your knees.

Last summer Dad brought me to "Bring
Your Child to Work Day" at his office. But
the people at Dad's work must've realized
their jobs would be boring to their kids, so
they brought in all sorts of entertainment.

For most of the day, us kids stayed in the cafeteria while the grown-ups got some work done in their offices.

Toward the end of the day, Dad brought me into his office while he tried to finish up an important project, so I sat there next to him and waited. But I think it was hard for him to concentrate while someone was looking over his shoulder.

Dad gave me money to buy something from the vending machine. He was probably just trying to get rid of me for a little while, so he wasn't too happy when I came back a minute later with a box of jawbreakers.

Dad told me he really needed to finish what he was doing, so he asked me to find somewhere else to sit while he wrapped things up. He must've been really distracted that day, though, because he went home and left me behind. I might've been stuck there all night if the janitor hadn't found me.

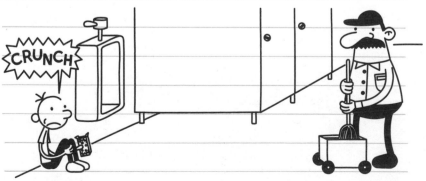

Anyway, Dad is pretty annoyed that Uncle Gary doesn't have any money and has been mooching off him. Mom has actually started giving Uncle Gary an allowance even though he doesn't have to do any chores for it, which feels wrong to me.

I just hope Uncle Gary uses some of his allowance to pay for his own bubble bath. He used up all of mine on the second day he was here, and it's really not the same when the water is crystal clear.

<u>Tuesday</u>

I really wish I didn't have to throw my
jeans out a few weeks ago, because today
at school I needed to look sharp. We're
starting a ballroom dancing unit in Phys
Ed, and Mrs. Moretta said each of us
needed to find a partner.

So it wasn't a good day to be wearing
corduroy pants that are three inches too short.

SHWEE
SHWEE
SHWEE

Mrs. Moretta said we were gonna choose
partners by writing down the name of the
person we wanted to dance with on a little
slip of paper. Then she'd go through the
pieces of paper and pair us up the best she
could. That was the same system she used
LAST year for the square dancing unit,
though, and I totally got burned.

I wrote down the name of the prettiest girl in my class, Baylee Anthony.

BAYLEE
ANTHONY

But she didn't write down MY name. She wrote down Bryce Anderson, just like every other girl in the class. Bryce ended up picking McKenzie Pollard, and Mrs. Moretta assigned Baylee to be my dance partner because I'd picked her.

At first I was really excited I got Baylee as a partner. But then I had to deal with THIS kind of nonsense for three weeks —

I guess Baylee didn't want a repeat of last year, either, because today she went around to all the guys who didn't have a chance with her and let them know.

To be honest with you, I don't really care who I get paired up with as long as it isn't Ruby Bird.

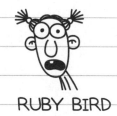

RUBY BIRD

As far as I know, Ruby is the only girl who has ever been suspended from our school, and that was for biting a teacher.

In fact, the reason Ruby only has one front tooth is because the other one ended up in Mr. Underwood's elbow.

I try to be pretty nice to Ruby whenever I come across her in the hallway, because she terrifies me.

But today I got worried that maybe I've been TOO nice and she might think I actually LIKE her. The last thing I need is for Ruby to write my name down on that little slip of paper, because I know if she's my dance partner, I'll do SOMETHING to make her mad and end up with her other tooth in MY arm.

So I used my little slip of paper to try and make sure that doesn't happen.

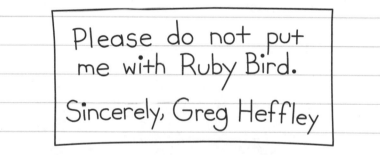

Please do not put me with Ruby Bird.
Sincerely, Greg Heffley

I even threw in a half-eaten candy bar I was saving for later on to make sure Mrs. Moretta comes through for me.

Wednesday
Last night I prayed extra hard that I wouldn't end up with Ruby as my dance partner.

Then I started worrying that maybe you only get a certain number of prayers answered in your lifetime and I'm burning through mine too fast. I'd hate to find out later on that I used up all my chits, because I've been acting like I've got an unlimited supply.

I probably need to be more careful about that. This weekend the toilet in the upstairs bathroom got clogged, and I prayed that the plumber wouldn't use our bathroom after he fixed it.

For the record, I have about a 75% success rate with my prayers. I don't know if that's good or bad, but one thing I'm pretty sure of is that I'm never gonna get a lightsaber for my birthday, no matter how badly I want it.

Anyway, I think I've got to be a lot more specific when I pray for something, because today in Phys Ed my wish was granted, but I'm not happy about the way things turned out.

At the beginning of class, Mrs. Moretta called out names for dance partners, and I held my breath when she got to Ruby Bird.

But Ruby got paired up with Fregley, and if you ask me, that's a match made in heaven.

Eventually, Mrs. Moretta read out the last girl's name, and there were still a bunch of boys left over, including me. There are a lot more boys in my class this year than girls, so it made sense that not everyone got a partner.

But still, I was a little disappointed that no one wrote my name on one of those little slips of paper.

Then us guys realized we weren't gonna have to do the ballroom dancing unit and that we could just play kickball on the other side of the gym for three weeks.

But we celebrated a little too soon. Mrs. Moretta said that EVERYONE had to dance, and she started pairing us boys up with ONE ANOTHER. So the next thing I knew, I was dancing a waltz with Carlos Escalera.

<u>Monday</u>
Today at school, Phys Ed was canceled
because we had a general assembly during
fourth period. I have to admit I was a little
disappointed when I found out, because
believe it or not, me and Carlos have actually
been getting the hang of the merengue.

Most people were pretty excited, though,
because we haven't had a general assembly
since November. That's when this
hypnotist called the Amazing Andrew came
to our school.

In the grand finale of his show, the Amazing
Andrew hypnotized a line of eighth-graders
into thinking their arms were superglued
together.

72

Then he told the guys he'd unglue them with a magic word, and when he said it they came apart just like that.

After school some kids got into an argument over whether the hypnotist was for real or if those eighth-graders were in on the act and just faking it.

Two of the kids who thought the Amazing
Andrew was a fake linked their arms, and
then Martin Ford tried to hypnotize them
into thinking they were superglued
together.

Believe it or not, it WORKED. The two
kids couldn't separate their arms, and they
totally panicked. Martin tried saying the
magic word, but he couldn't unstick them.

The kids went back to the school, and one of the teachers had to track down the Amazing Andrew at his job so he could say the magic word and separate them.

I have no idea how the school chooses the people who come in and do our assemblies. One person they brought in last year was a guy called Strong Steve. He gave a speech about how we needed to stay off drugs, and then for his grand finale he ripped a phone book in half with his bare hands.

Don't ask me what ripping a phone book has to do with staying off drugs, but the kids at my school went crazy for this guy. In fact, the librarian had to replace half the reference books on our shelves after Strong Steve's visit.

The person I'm really hoping they DON'T bring back is this singer named Krisstina. I think the school likes to bring in Krisstina for assemblies because her lyrics are really positive.

Krisstina calls herself an "international pop sensation," but I don't know how she gets away with that. As far as I can tell, she's never even been out of the STATE.

One of my favorite assemblies was the one where a police officer came to our school and told us about being a "narc." He said his job was to pose as a high school student and then report on the kids who were up to no good.

I thought that sounded like an AWESOME job. If I can get paid to go to school without doing homework or taking tests AND send all the jerks to jail, then that's the career for me.

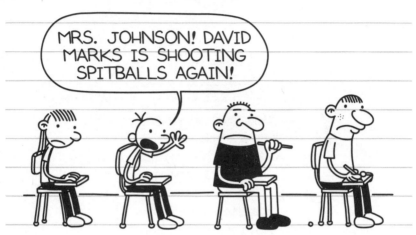

After the police officer came to our school, me and my friend Rowley decided to start our own detective agency.

Unfortunately, there wasn't a lot of demand for private detectives in our neighborhood, and nobody wanted to hire us. But we decided to start spying on people ANYWAY.

It was actually a lot of fun. The great thing about being a private investigator is that you can poke around in other people's lives and it's just part of your job.

We mostly focused our investigations on Mr. Millis, who lives a few doors up the street from me. It's not like he was doing anything suspicious. It's just that we knew he had all the movie channels on cable.

Our detective agency fell apart, though, after we started investigating Scotty Douglas. I'd let him borrow a video game over the summer and he said he lost it, but I knew he was lying. So I sent Rowley down to Scotty's house to get him to cough it up.

I taught Rowley how to act really tough and crack his knuckles a lot so Scotty would get the message that we weren't fooling around.

But when Rowley didn't come back right
away, I started to wonder what happened.
I went down to Scotty's house myself
to investigate, and I caught Rowley red-
handed playing my video game with Scotty.

I had to fire Rowley on the spot, and if I
ever start another detective agency, the
first thing I'm gonna do is hire a more
intimidating enforcer.

Anyway, like I said, everyone was excited
to find out who the guest was for today's
assembly.

But it turned out there WASN'T a guest.
After we sat down in the gym, Vice
Principal Roy got up on the stage and
said the reason he gathered us all together
was to announce that there was gonna be
a special election to replace the student
council.

We had student council elections in the
fall. But the class officers were skipping
the meetings because they're held during
recess, and I guess the advisors got fed up.

Vice Principal Roy said there are two
conditions for running for office. One, you
have to be willing to attend all the student
council meetings. And two, you can't have
three detentions or more.

I felt like that second rule was directed at ME, because I just picked up my third detention.

In my first year of middle school, an eighth-grader told me there was a secret elevator that went to the second floor, and that he could sell me a special pass for five bucks.

That sounded like a good deal to ME, so I gave him five dollars for the pass, which looked pretty official.

ELEVATOR PASS

This pass entitles the
holder to unlimited use of
the middle school elevator.

But it turned out the whole thing was a
scam and there was no such thing as a
secret elevator.

I'd been holding on to that elevator pass
ever since. But a few weeks ago I sold it to a
kid who's new to our school.

Unfortunately, I wasn't careful enough, and
I got busted by Vice Principal Roy, who
made me return the money.

He even gave me a detention, which really stunk, because I'd given the kid a deal by selling him the pass at half price.

After the assembly I realized something: Rowley has never had a detention, so he'd be the PERFECT candidate for student council. I told him he should run, but he said he wouldn't know what he'd do if he got elected.

But that's where I come in. I told him if he gets elected, I'll make all the tough decisions and all he'll have to do is show up for the meetings and do what I tell him. I think it's a GENIUS idea, because I'll get to be in power but I won't have to miss any recess.

I volunteered to be his campaign manager so he won't even have to lift a finger to get elected. So we went to the bulletin board in the front hallway to sign Rowley up.

I told him he should run for one of the juicy spots like President or Vice President, but he wanted to run for "Social Chairperson." I have no idea what a Social Chairperson does, but as long as Rowley gets to vote on the important decisions, I'm fine with it.

Wednesday
Yesterday some of the other candidates were hanging posters up in the hallways and handing out buttons and candy to get themselves elected. So we were ALREADY behind.

86

I knew I was gonna have to dream up something big to make sure Rowley gets elected, so here's what I came up with.

When the candidates give their speeches in the gym, the bleachers will be full of students. At sports games I've seen on TV, people in the stadium paint their chests to spell out messages.

Last night I got a bunch of Uncle Gary's T-shirts from the garage, turned them inside out, and wrote a letter on each one so they spelled out "VOTE ROWLEY JEFFERSON FOR SOCIAL CHAIRPERSON." It took all night, and I went through about twenty markers, but I knew it was gonna make a big splash at the assembly.

I got to school early today and gave each kid who was willing to wear a shirt a piece of bubble gum.

But when we got into the gym, getting the kids to stand in the right order was like trying to herd cats.

88

The only candidates who got to give speeches were the ones who were running for President. I was pretty relieved to hear that, because when I had Rowley rehearse his speech for Social Chairperson, he was a nervous wreck.

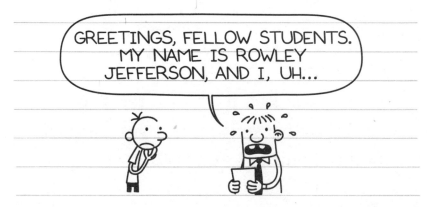

GREETINGS, FELLOW STUDENTS. MY NAME IS ROWLEY JEFFERSON, AND I, UH...

The first candidate to give a speech was a girl named Sydney Greene who is a straight-A student and has never missed a day of school. She said that if she's elected President, she'll get better equipment for the music room and will organize a project to put new protective covers on the books in the library.

Next up was Bryan Buttsy. As soon as Vice Principal Roy called Bryan up to the podium, everyone in the gym started making all sorts of obnoxious noises.

I'm sure Bryan said a lot of interesting things during his speech, but you couldn't hear a word with all that racket.

I just hope Bryan doesn't run for President when he's a grown-up, because if he does, his campaign rallies are gonna be RIDICULOUS.

The last candidate to go was a kid named Eugene Ellis. Eugene is the only person running for President who didn't put up posters or hand out lollipops or anything like that, so nobody really took him seriously.

Eugene's campaign speech was only about thirty seconds long. He said that if he's elected President, he'll get the school to replace the cheap toilet paper in the bathrooms with the expensive, quilted kind.

When Eugene finished his speech, the whole place went berserk. Kids are ALWAYS complaining about the toilet paper situation because the type the school uses is like sandpaper.

And from the reaction Eugene got, I don't think Sydney or Bryan has a prayer.

Thursday
Just like I predicted, Eugene Ellis won student council President by a landslide. Rowley won, too, because he was the only person who actually signed up for Social Chairperson. I wish I'd known that, because I could've saved myself a lot of hassle with those T-shirts.

The student council had their first meeting today, and Mrs. Birch, the teacher who works with the council, told Eugene the school couldn't afford to stock the bathrooms with quilted toilet paper, so he might as well forget about it.

Word got around school fast, and people were pretty mad. The whole reason everyone voted for Eugene was because of his campaign promise. Plus, we do fundraisers for the school every year, and you would think they could take some of the money we make and spend it on some quality toilet paper.

I thought the school would be rolling in dough after the LAST fundraiser we had a few weeks ago, when we sold candy bars. I have to give credit to whoever came up with the idea. The school sent each student home with fifty Chocolate Crunch candy bars, and we were supposed to go out and sell them to our neighbors.

But I don't know a single kid who didn't eat at least three or four candy bars before they even got home. In fact, I ate fifteen by the time Mom found out and put a stop to it.

So a lot of families like mine had to write a check to the school just to cover the cost of the candy bars their children ate. It's possible that nobody sold a single candy bar during that fundraiser.

Saturday
Speaking of money, Uncle Gary spent all of his allowance this week and asked me if he could borrow some of MINE. When Dad found out, he was pretty mad.

It turns out Uncle Gary spent his money on scratch tickets at the convenience store. Dad told Uncle Gary he's got a better chance of getting struck by lightning than winning the lottery and that he's just wasting his money.

Dad probably should've chosen his words more carefully, because now Manny won't step foot outside if it's raining.

Scratch tickets are a sore subject for Dad
anyway. A few years ago Dad bought Uncle
Gary a nice winter jacket for Christmas,
and Uncle Gary gave Dad a scratch ticket.
Dad seemed a little annoyed that he'd spent
all that money on Uncle Gary and Uncle
Gary just gave him a gift that only cost a
buck.

Dad scratched off the little squares on the
card with a coin and he got three cherries,
which meant he'd just won a hundred
thousand dollars.

But it turned out the ticket was just a gag
gift, and it was a fake.

We still can't mention that Christmas to Dad, because it just puts him in a bad mood for the rest of the day.

What Dad REALLY wants is for Uncle Gary to get a job so he can move out of our house. I'm starting to wish Uncle Gary would get a job, too, because lately he's been spending a lot of time in my room playing on the computer.

He's addicted to this virtual-world game where you can be anything you want, like a policeman or a construction worker or a rock star.

But in the game, Uncle Gary is just a guy who doesn't have a job and buys a bunch of scratch tickets every day.

FEBRUARY

<u>Thursday</u>
There have been some pretty big developments at school this week.

It all started on Monday at the last student council meeting. The meetings are held in the teachers lounge, and after the Treasurer, Javan Hill, went to use the bathroom, he came out with a roll of Pillow-Soft Ultra toilet paper.

That means the teachers have been treating themselves to good toilet paper while us kids are stuck with the cheap stuff.

When Eugene Ellis confronted Mrs. Birch, she knew the teachers were totally busted.

Mrs. Birch said that even though the teachers use Pillow-Soft Ultra, there's not enough money in the budget to stock all the kids' bathrooms with expensive toilet paper, but she could agree to a compromise.

She said the school could allow kids to bring in their OWN rolls from home. And when the announcement came over the loudspeaker, it was a huge victory for Eugene Ellis and the rest of the student council.

Tuesday was the first day kids were allowed to bring in their own toilet paper, and I think some people went a little overboard.

In fact, some kids brought in so much toilet paper that there wasn't enough room to fit it in their lockers, so they carried their supply around with them.

Everything probably would've been just fine, but at lunch someone threw a roll of toilet paper at somebody else, and within about fifteen seconds it was a total madhouse.

Later that afternoon the principal got on the loudspeaker and said that from now on, we're only allowed to bring five squares of toilet paper to school a day. That seems like a pretty ridiculous rule, because I don't know ANYONE who can get by on five squares.

Yesterday a few kids got caught bringing in more than they were supposed to, so now the teachers are checking our bags when we come in through the front doors in the morning.

SHAKE SHAKE

Thursday
By the time the principal set that five-square limit last week, I'd already stocked my locker with about twenty rolls.

102

The teachers do random checks on kids' lockers now, and I knew sooner or later they were gonna find my secret stash.

I wanted to make sure my supply lasted to the end of the school year, so I needed to figure out how to protect it.

I decided the only way to do THAT was to have a stall in the bathroom all to myself, and to keep my toilet paper hidden in there.

So on Monday I picked a stall that was pretty clean and locked the door. Then I crawled underneath it to get out.

Next I slipped some old sneakers I brought from home on the floor in front of the toilet to make it look like the stall was occupied.

Every time I needed to use the bathroom this week, I waited to make sure no one was around, then I crawled underneath my stall door. It was like I had a tiny little apartment in there. In fact, I wish I'd thought of this idea a long time ago.

For a few days my system worked great. No one even TRIED to use my private stall.

But then I forgot to pick one of the spare shoes up off the ground, and I guess that must've looked pretty suspicious from the outside.

It wasn't long before people figured out I was hoarding quality toilet paper, and things fell apart pretty quickly after that.

<u>Friday</u>
I think what the students learned from the toilet paper experience is that if we want something, we're gonna have to raise the money on our own.

So last week the student council brainstormed ideas for a class fundraiser. The Vice President, Hillary Pine, said we should have a car wash, and the Secretary, Olivia Davis, said we should do a giant yard sale.

I thought we should sell caramel popcorn, but either Rowley didn't have his walkie-talkie up loud enough or everybody was just ignoring me.

Eugene Ellis suggested a pro wrestling match in the gym, and Javan Hill came up with the idea of a motocross stunt show. But they couldn't decide which idea they liked better, so they settled on a mixed motocross/wrestling event.

I think Eugene realized it was gonna take a
lot of work to pull something like that off, so
he assigned it to his Vice President. Hillary
formed a Fundraising Committee and got
her friends on the student council to join it.

On Monday, Hillary reported back to the
student council and said that everything
for the event was planned but that the
Fundraising Committee had made a few
"small changes" to the original idea.

Somehow the motocross/wrestling event
morphed into a VALENTINE'S DAY
dance. Eugene and the other guys wanted
to change it back, but Mrs. Birch said
they had to respect the decision of the
Fundraising Committee. I'm sure the truth
is that she wasn't really crazy about the idea
of motorized vehicles in the gym to begin
with.

Ever since word got out about the
Valentine's Day dance, it's all anyone can
talk about at school. The girls seem really
excited, and they're treating it like some
sort of middle school prom.

There's already a Dance Committee, which
Rowley got invited to be on since he's the
Social Chairperson. I'm just glad there's
some male representation on that committee,
because if the girls have their way, Krisstina
will be the entertainment for the night.

Most of the boys couldn't care less about
the dance. I've heard a bunch of guys
saying there's no way they're gonna pay
three bucks to go to a dance in the school
gymnasium. But that all changed earlier
this week when the first Candy Grams got
handed out in homeroom.

The Candy Grams are invitations to the Valentine's Day dance, and the Dance Committee started selling them at lunch the other day. If you pay twenty-five cents, you can send a Candy Gram to anyone you want, and Bryce Anderson got ones from at least five different girls right off the bat.

Dear Bryce,
It would be "sweet" if you'd go with me to the Valentine's Day dance!
Signed,
Jessica

After the first wave of Candy Grams got delivered, some of the boys who didn't get one got jealous of the guys who DID. Now all of a sudden EVERYONE wants to go to the dance because no one wants to be left out. So yesterday at lunch there was a big rush on Candy Grams.

Like I said before, there are more boys than girls in my grade this year, and I think a lot of guys are nervous they're not gonna end up with a date to the dance. So most of the boys are acting really different whenever a girl is around.

At lunch, guys usually take spoonfuls of mashed potatoes and flick them up at the ceiling to try and get them to stick.

Don't even ask me WHAT they put in the
potatoes that makes them stick like that.

Sometimes I forget to look up before I find
a place to sit.

The girls really hate the mashed potato
thing, and that's why they sit on the other
side of the cafeteria. But now the boys
know they're not gonna get one of the girls
to go with them to the dance if they act like
jerks.

112

I can tell it's hard for a lot of the boys to be mature in front of the girls. So some guys are acting out when there aren't any girls around.

We're in the middle of a basketball unit in Phys Ed, with the girls playing on one side of the gym and the boys on the other. The other day this kid named Anthony Renfrew thought it would be pretty funny if he pantsed Daniel Revis when he was shooting free throws.

Everybody laughed except for Daniel, but later on Daniel got Anthony back when he was going for a layup. After that it was a free-for-all, with everyone pantsing everyone else. So things have been AWFUL since then.

Now everyone's so paranoid about getting pantsed that no one will even stand up during our basketball scrimmages.

I've even started wearing two pairs of shorts under my sweatpants for extra insurance.

Things have gotten so bad that Vice Principal Roy came into the gym today to lecture the boys. He said this was no laughing matter and that anyone caught pantsing another student would be suspended.

But Vice Principal Roy should've watched where he was standing, because some kid snuck under the bleachers and got him pretty good.

Whoever did it escaped before Vice Principal Roy could catch him. No one knows for sure who it was, but the name they're using for the guy is the Mad Pantser.

Tuesday
It's been about a week since they introduced these Candy Grams, and I'm getting a little concerned that I haven't gotten one yet. I've never flung potatoes on the ceiling and I've never pantsed anyone in my life, so I don't know what a guy needs to do to impress a girl these days.

It seems like every guy in my homeroom
has gotten a Candy Gram. Even Travis
Hickey got one, and he'll eat a crust of
pizza out of a trash can if you give him a
quarter.

Uncle Gary was playing his computer game
in my room the other night, and I told him
about the Valentine's Day dance and the
Candy Grams. Believe it or not, he gave me
some really good advice.

Uncle Gary told me the best way to get a
girl's attention is by making yourself look
"unavailable." He said what I should do
is buy a bunch of Candy Grams and have
them all delivered to MYSELF so the girls
would think I was a really hot property.

I probably should've thought about talking to Uncle Gary a lot earlier. He's been married something like four times already, so he's an EXPERT on relationships.

Yesterday I bought two dollars' worth of Candy Grams, and today in homeroom they were delivered to me.

HERE'S ANOTHER ONE FOR GREG HEFFLEY!

YAWN!

I just hope this works, because that two bucks was my lunch money.

<u>Friday</u>
By Wednesday I'd blown through five dollars, and I realized if I kept buying Candy Grams for myself, I was gonna starve to death. So I decided to actually buy a Candy Gram for a GIRL and see how that went.

Yesterday at lunch I bought a Candy Gram and sent it to Adrianne Simpson, who sits three rows away from me in English. But I didn't want to risk my whole quarter on one person, so I made sure I got my money's worth.

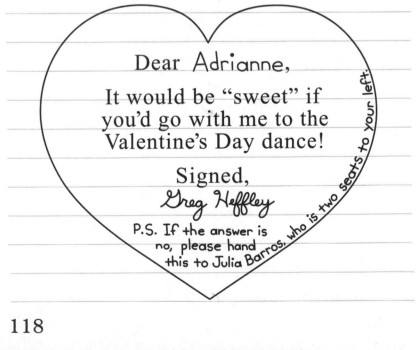

Dear Adrianne,

It would be "sweet" if you'd go with me to the Valentine's Day dance!

Signed,
Greg Heffley

P.S. If the answer is no, please hand this to Julia Barros, who is two seats to your left.

Adrianne and Julia were both giving me dirty looks when I walked into class today, so I'm assuming it's a no from both of them.

I realized a Candy Gram isn't the ONLY way to ask a girl to a dance, though. There's a girl named Leighann Marlow who sits in the same chair for homeroom that I sit in for History class. So I wrote her a note on my desk, and it didn't cost me a cent.

Unfortunately, I forgot that after-school detention is held in the same room as History, so some moron jumped in with an answer before Leighann even had a chance to read my note.

Hi Leighann-
If you are looking
for someone to go
to the dance with,
just let me know
by writing back.

Greg Heffley

Hi Greg- I am sorry
but I'm not interested in
going to the dance with you.
Leighann

Dear Greg
Yes I will go to
the dance with you
and P.S. will you marry
me?

KISS
KISS

HAR HAR
HAR

I'm pretty nervous, because it seems like there aren't really a lot of girls left to choose from at this point.

One girl who doesn't have a date yet is Erika Hernandez. She just broke up with her boyfriend, this kid named Jamar Law, who is famous in our school for getting his head stuck in a chair. The janitor even had to cut him free with a hacksaw. It's in the yearbook and everything.

Sticky situation: Jamar Law gets a little help from Mr. Lewis after getting his head stuck in a chair during Mrs. Moran's art class.

Erika is really pretty and nice, so don't ask me what she was thinking when she started going out with a doofus like Jamar.

She WOULD be at the top of my list for the dance. But I'm worried that if things worked out between me and her, I'd always be thinking about her ex-boyfriend and I wouldn't be able to get past it.

The Erika Hernandez situation has made me wonder what other girls might have a Jamar Law in their past. It's hard to keep track of who has gone out with who in my school, and that's important information when you're looking for a date to the dance. So I drew up a chart to see how everyone in my grade is connected.

I've still got a long way to go, but here's the incomplete version.

The person I'm worried about is a boy named Evan Whitehead. I've heard him bragging that he's kissed a bunch of different girls in my grade.

But last week he got sent home from school because he had the chicken pox, which I didn't even know you could still GET anymore. So who knows HOW many girls Evan's infected.

One girl I'm pretty sure Evan never kissed is Julie Webber, because she's been going out with Ed Norwell since the fifth grade. But I've heard their relationship is a little shaky these days, so I'm gonna do what I can to help speed things along.

<u>Tuesday</u>
Uncle Gary told me that if I want a girl to go to the dance with me, I'm gonna have to ask her face-to-face. I've been trying to avoid that, but I think he's probably right.

There's a girl named Peyton Ellis who I've always kind of had a crush on, and when I saw her drinking from the water fountain yesterday, I stood there and waited patiently for her to finish. But Peyton must've seen me out of the corner of her eye and realized I was gonna ask her to the dance, so she just kept drinking and drinking while I stood there like a dope.

Eventually, the bell rang and we both had to go to class.

I barely know Peyton, so maybe it was a bad idea to try and ask her anyway. I realized I should probably stick with girls who I've got some kind of a connection with. The first person to come to mind was Bethany Breen, my lab partner in Science.

But I don't think I've made such a good impression on Bethany. We're in the middle of our anatomy unit, and for the past few days we've been dissecting frogs. I'm really squeamish when it comes to that sort of thing, so I just let Bethany do the dissecting while I stand on the other side of the room trying not to throw up.

Seriously, though, in this day and age I don't know why we're still cutting open frogs to see what's inside them.

If somebody tells me there's a heart and intestines inside a frog, I'm willing to take their word for it.

I was pretty happy I got paired up with Bethany as lab partners. I remember back in elementary school, whenever a teacher picked a boy and a girl to do something together, all the other kids would go CRAZY.

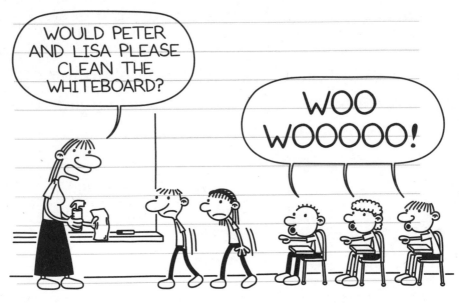

When I got picked to be lab partners with Bethany, I was hoping for some kind of reaction from the rest of the class. But I guess everyone's outgrown that stuff.

Even though I haven't impressed Bethany with my dissection skills, I still thought I might have a shot with her. I don't want to brag or anything, but I HAVE been a pretty hilarious lab partner.

At the end of the day yesterday, I walked up to Bethany when she was getting her coat out of her locker.

I admit I was a little nervous talking to her even though we spend forty-five minutes every day as lab partners. But before I got a single word out, I started thinking about the frogs. So I don't think it's gonna work out between me and her.

Last night when I was telling Uncle Gary about what happened at school, he said my problem is that I'm trying to do this on my own and I need a "wingman" to help me look good in front of the girls so it's easier to ask one out.

Well, I think Rowley would be a PERFECT wingman for me, because he makes me look good just by being himself.

Today I asked Rowley to be my wingman, but he didn't really understand the concept. So I told him it's just like being my campaign manager, but for the dance.

Rowley said maybe we could be EACH OTHER's wingman and help each other get a date to the dance, but I said we should do this one person at a time. I feel like we need to get my situation taken care of first, because getting Rowley a date to the dance could end up being a long-term project.

We gave the wingman thing a trial run at lunch, but I think there's still a lot of room for improvement.

I HEARD GREG HEFFLEY HAS REALLY STRONG MUSCLES.

Thursday

On the walk home from school today, Rowley told me he heard from a girl on the Dance Committee that Alyssa Grove just broke up with her boyfriend and is looking for a date to the dance.

See, that's EXACTLY why I made Rowley my wingman. Alyssa is one of the most popular girls in my school, so I was gonna have to act quick before one of the other goobers in my class got to her.

When I got home I called Alyssa's number right away, but no one was there. The answering machine picked up really fast, and the next thing I knew I was leaving a message.

UM...YES...THIS IS GREG HEFFLEY SPEAKING...AND, UH, I'M CALLING REGARDING, UM...

I hit the "pound" key on the phone so I could delete my message and start over. But my second message wasn't that great, either.

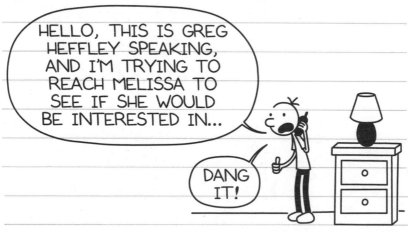

HELLO, THIS IS GREG HEFFLEY SPEAKING, AND I'M TRYING TO REACH MELISSA TO SEE IF SHE WOULD BE INTERESTED IN...

DANG IT!

I must've recorded twenty messages, because I wanted to get it just right. But Rowley was in the room with me trying to stay completely silent, and whenever I looked at him I just completely lost it.

After a while me and Rowley were just totally having fun and goofing around.

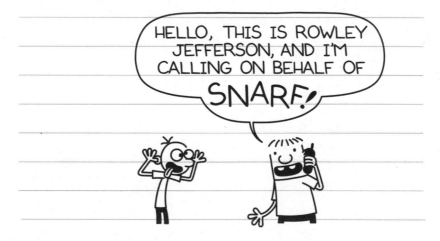

I knew there was no way I could leave a serious message while Rowley was at my house, so I deleted the last one and hung up the phone. I figured I might as well just wait until tomorrow morning and talk to Alyssa in person.

But what I didn't know was that hitting the "pound" key didn't delete my messages on the Groves' voice mail system the way it does on ours. So after dinner tonight there was a knock on the door, and it was Alyssa's father.

Mr. Grove told Dad that me and my friend had left twenty prank messages on his machine and that he'd appreciate it if we never called his house again.

So I guess I'm gonna have to scratch Alyssa off my list.

<u>Monday</u>
Uncle Gary told me if I really want to
send the right signals to girls at school, I
might consider updating my wardrobe. He
said that wearing a new shirt or new shoes
always makes him feel more confident, and
it might work for me, too.

The thing is, I really don't HAVE a lot
of new clothes. I'd say about 90% of
everything I wear is a hand-me-down
from Rodrick. Mom would say that's an
exaggeration, but all you have to do is
check the tags in my underwear for proof.

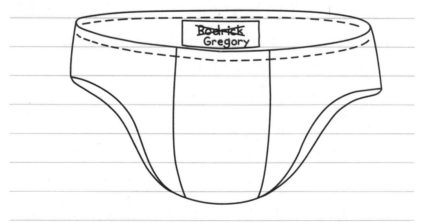

I never really cared much about what I wore,
but now Uncle Gary has me wondering if
my wardrobe is holding me back.

This weekend I asked Mom if we could go out and get me some new jeans and shoes so I could really look sharp at school, but the minute I said it I wished I could take it back.

Mom gave me a long speech about how kids in middle school focus too much on appearances, and how if we spent half the time on academics that we do on deciding what to wear, our country wouldn't be ranked twenty-fifth in the world in math.

I should've known Mom wouldn't run right out and buy me a whole bunch of new clothes. In fact, when Mom was on the PTA, she started a petition pushing for school uniforms because she'd read some article that said kids who wear uniforms do better in academics.

Luckily, she didn't get enough signatures, but word got around that my mom was the one who started the school uniform petition, and there was a stretch of a few weeks where I had to wait a half hour at the end of each day before it was safe to walk home.

Since Mom wouldn't take me out clothes shopping, I decided to start poking around the house to see if there was anything cool I could wear.

I started by going through Rodrick's dresser drawers, but I don't think we have the same taste when it comes to clothes.

136

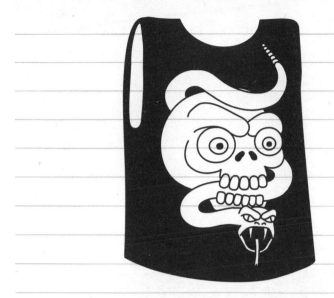

Uncle Gary told me I should look in Dad's closet, because sometimes grown-ups have "vintage" stuff that looks cool. I've never seen Dad wear anything cool in my whole life, but I was willing to give it a try.

I'm glad Uncle Gary gave me that tip, because believe it or not, I found EXACTLY what I was looking for in the back of Dad's closet.

It was a BLACK LEATHER JACKET.
I've never seen Dad wear it, so I figured he
must've bought it before I was born.

I had no idea Dad owned anything that
cool, and it kind of made me see him in a
whole new light.

I put it on and went downstairs. Dad
seemed pretty surprised to see his old
leather jacket, and he said he bought it back
when he was first dating Mom.

I asked Dad if I could borrow it, and he said he didn't need it anymore so it was OK by him.

Unfortunately, Mom wasn't on board with the idea. She said the jacket was way too expensive for a middle school student to wear and that I might damage it or lose it.

I told her that wasn't fair, because it was just sitting in the closet gathering dust, so it didn't really matter if something happened to it. But Mom said the jacket sent the "wrong message" and that, besides, it wasn't a winter coat. So she told me to put it back in the upstairs closet.

But when I was in the shower this morning, I just couldn't stop thinking about how awesome it would be to wear that thing to school. I knew I could probably sneak it out of the house and put it back in the closet later without Mom even noticing.

So while she was feeding Manny breakfast, I went upstairs, grabbed the jacket, and slipped out the front door.

The first thing I have to say is, Mom was right about the jacket not being a winter coat.

That thing didn't have any sort of lining, and halfway to school I was starting to really regret my decision.

My gloves were in my winter coat at home, and my hands were FREEZING. So I shoved them in the pockets of the jacket, but there was something in each one.

There was a really cool pair of aviator sunglasses in one of the pockets, so that was a bonus. In the other there was one of those picture strips you get at a photo booth in the mall.

At first I didn't recognize the people in the picture, but then I realized it was Mom and Dad.

I really wish I hadn't seen that right after eating breakfast.

When I got to school, every head turned in my direction as I walked down the hallway.

In fact, I got so much attention that I decided to keep the jacket on the rest of the day. I felt like a whole new person in homeroom.

A few minutes before the bell rang to start the day, there was a loud knocking on the little window in the door.

I just about had a heart attack when I saw
who it was.

When the teacher opened the door, Mom
walked straight to my desk and made me
hand over Dad's leather jacket in front of
everyone.

I told Mom it was too cold outside for me
to walk home without a jacket, so she gave
me HER winter coat to wear.

I wasn't too happy about the situation, but at least I was warm on the way home.

Wednesday

By now everybody at school has heard about the guy whose Mom made him wear her winter coat. So this is gonna make it a lot harder for me to find a date to the dance.

That's why I've decided my best shot is to take someone who DOESN'T go to my school to the dance. And I think I've found the perfect place to look: church.

I've heard that the students at the church school think the kids who go to public school are pretty tough. So whenever I run into one of my friends at church, I make sure to play it real cool in front of the church kids.

Recently, Mom has become friends with Mrs. Stringer at church because they both worked on the Fall Fair Committee.

The Stringers have two kids who go to the church school, a boy named Wesley and a girl named Laurel. I've never actually seen Wesley, so he must be down in the basement with the other little kids during church.

MR.   LAUREL   MRS.
STRINGER   STRINGER   STRINGER

A few nights ago Mom invited the whole Stringer family over to our house for dinner this Friday. I think she's hoping Manny and Wesley will click and Manny can be friends with a real live person for once.

But I can see a real opportunity here for ME. Laurel is in my grade, and she's better looking than most of the girls in my class. So this dinner could really change my fortunes.

<u>Friday</u>

Mom spent a long time getting the house ready before the Stringers came over, and when I took a look around, I realized I'd better pitch in, too.

There were embarrassing things all over the place. For starters, we still had our Christmas tree up in the living room. It was too much work to dismantle it, so me and Dad just shoved it in the garage.

There were diapers taped on all the corners of our family room furniture that were left over from when Mom baby-proofed the house after Manny started crawling.

She used packing tape to hold the diapers in place, and THAT wasn't easy to get off.

Uncle Gary was on the couch in the family room taking a nap, so we just covered him with a sheet and hoped nobody would want to sit there.

Next was the kitchen. There's a bulletin board on the wall with different certificates and ribbons that Mom has given us kids over the years.

Everything with my name on it is really lame, so I took it off the wall and hid it in the pantry.

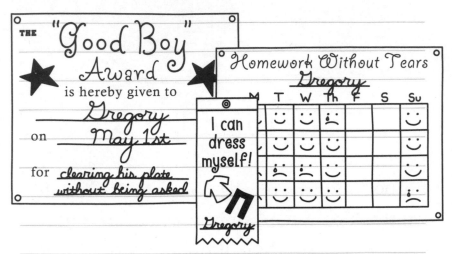

By the time the Stringers showed up, we'd taken care of all the major stuff. But the visit got off to a really shaky start. You remember how I said Manny was afraid of some kid at church who acted like a vampire? Well, it turns out that kid was Wesley Stringer.

So any hope Mom had of Manny making a new friend was completely out the window. Manny skipped dinner and spent the rest of the night hiding in his bedroom, which I wish I could've done, because Mom made a fancy meal to impress our guests.

It was cream of mushroom chicken with asparagus on top. I know asparagus is supposed to be really good for you, but to me it's like kryptonite.

I didn't want to look unsophisticated in front of Laurel, though, so I decided to just close my eyes, plug my nose, and choke it down.

The grown-ups talked about politics and stuff that wasn't all that interesting, and me and Laurel just had to sit there and listen.

Mom told Mrs. Stringer about some fancy restaurant she goes to with Dad when they have a "date night," and Mrs. Stringer said that she and her husband can never go out for dinner on weekends because Laurel is always off doing something with friends and they can't find a reliable babysitter for Wesley.

I told Mrs. Stringer that if they ever need a babysitter, they should call ME.

I figured it's a way to get in good with the Stringers and get paid doing it. Mom liked the idea, too, and she said babysitting would be a great experience for me. Mrs. Stringer seemed pretty impressed, and she asked if I was free tomorrow, so I told her I was.

I don't want to get too far ahead of myself here, but I'm sure one day I'll be sitting around with the Stringers on Thanksgiving and we'll all be laughing about how I used to babysit my brother-in-law, Wesley, when I was in middle school.

Saturday
Tonight Mom dropped me off at the Stringers' house at 6:30.

Mrs. Stringer said Laurel had already gone to a friend's house, which kind of stunk, because I was hoping I might get to see her for a few minutes and talk to her about the dance.

Mrs. Stringer said I should put Wesley to bed at 8:00 and that they'd be home around 9:00. She told me I could watch TV until they got home and to help myself to anything in the fridge.

After Mr. and Mrs. Stringer left, it was just me and Wesley. I asked Wesley if he wanted to play a board game or something like that, but he said he wanted to go out in the garage and get his bike.

I told him it was too cold to ride his bike outside, but he said he wanted to ride it INSIDE. The Stringers have a really nice house, and I was pretty sure they didn't want Wesley scratching up their hardwood floors. So I told him we needed to find something else to do.

Wesley had a huge fit. After he calmed down he told me he wanted to color instead. I asked him where his coloring stuff was, and he said it was in the laundry room. But when I went to get it, I heard the latch on the door lock behind me.

Then I heard the garage door open, and the next thing I knew Wesley was riding around the kitchen on his bike.

I pounded on the door for him to let me out, but he just ignored me.

Next I heard the basement door open, and then a rumbling sound followed by a HUGE crash. I could hear Wesley crying at the bottom of the stairs, and I started to panic because it sounded like he was really hurt.

But then Wesley calmed down, and I could hear him dragging his bike back up to the top of the stairs. Then he rode down the stairs and crashed at the bottom AGAIN, followed by MORE tears.

I am not exaggerating when I tell you this went on for an hour and a half. I thought Wesley would wear himself out, but he never did. I remembered that the Stringers said they couldn't find a babysitter for Wesley, and now that was starting to make a lot of sense.

I figured I was gonna have to punish Wesley for locking me in the laundry room once I got out of there. What he DESERVED was a good spanking, but I figured that probably wouldn't fly with the Stringers.

I decided I'd give Wesley a time-out, because that's what my parents always did when I misbehaved as a little kid. In fact, when I was little I even got time-outs from RODRICK.

The thing is, I had no idea Rodrick didn't actually have the AUTHORITY to give me time-outs. And I can't tell you how many hours I logged in that time-out chair when Rodrick was babysitting me.

One time I was throwing a ball in the house while I was home alone with Rodrick, and I accidentally knocked over a wedding photo of Mom and Dad. Rodrick gave me a half-hour time-out for THAT one.

When Mom and Dad got home, they saw the broken picture and asked which one of us had done it. I told them it was me but that they didn't need to give me a punishment, because I'd already gotten a time-out from RODRICK.

But Mom said the only people who could hand out punishments were her and Dad, so I ended up serving a DOUBLE time-out for breaking that picture.

I figured Wesley deserved a TRIPLE time-out for locking me in the laundry room. But it was getting pretty late, and I knew it would look bad if the Stringers came home and I was still locked inside.

So I started looking for another way out. There was a spare freezer blocking a door to the back deck, so I pushed with all my might and gave myself just enough room to squeeze through and open the door.

It was really cold outside, and I was only wearing a T-shirt and pants. I tried to open the front door, but it was locked.

I decided if I was gonna catch this kid off guard, I'd need the element of surprise. So I walked around the house and tried all the windows on the first floor until I found one that was unlocked. I then pushed it open and crawled inside.

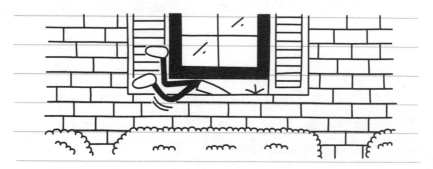

I landed headfirst in someone's bedroom, and after I looked around I realized it must be Laurel's.

Like I said, it was freezing cold outside, so I needed to warm up before going after Wesley. But I really regret taking a few minutes to do that, because in the time I was in Laurel's room, Mr. and Mrs. Stringer came home.

AAAHHH...

Hopefully, we can all have a good chuckle about this story at some future Thanksgiving, too. But I think it's gonna be a while before Mr. Stringer is ready to laugh about this one.

Wednesday
After blowing my chances with Laurel Stringer, I pretty much gave up on finding someone to take to the dance. It's only three days away, and by now everyone who's going is already paired up with someone else. So I figured I'd be spending Saturday night at home playing video games by myself.

But yesterday Rowley gave me some news after one of his Dance Committee meetings that changed EVERYTHING.

He said Abigail Brown was upset during the meeting because the boy she was going with, Michael Sampson, has a family obligation and had to cancel on her. So now Abigail has a dress and no one to go to the dance with.

So the stage is set for me to swoop in and be the hero. I told Rowley this was his big chance to come through as my wingman and hook me up with Abigail.

The thing is, Abigail doesn't really know me, and I kind of doubted she'd go to the dance with a person she doesn't know. So I told Rowley he should tell Abigail the three of us could go to the dance TOGETHER as a "group of friends."

Rowley seemed to like that idea because he's been doing all this work on the Dance Committee and didn't have anyone to go with, either.

164

I figured the three of us could go out to dinner, and at the restaurant Abigail would get to see what a great guy I was. By the time we got to the dance, we'd walk in as a couple.

The only problem was that we'd need a RIDE. I wasn't about to ask Mom for one, because the seats in our minivan are crusted with old Cheerios and God knows what else. Plus, having Mom along on my date could be a total disaster.

I knew if I really wanted to impress Abigail, I'd need to rent a limo, but those things cost a FORTUNE. Then I had an idea.

Rowley's dad has a really nice car, so I figured we could get HIM to drive us. Abigail wouldn't even have to know Mr. Jefferson was Rowley's dad. If we didn't say anything, she'd just think he was a professional driver. Maybe I'll even get him one of those hats chauffeurs wear, to really sell the idea.

Of course, we wouldn't be able to say anything to MR. JEFFERSON, either. Me and him kind of have a bad history, and I'm sure he wouldn't be looking to do me any extra favors.

Things started falling into place today. Rowley talked to Abigail, and she likes the whole "group of friends" idea. And on top of that, Mr. Jefferson agreed to drive us to the dance.

166

So now I'm keeping my fingers crossed that nothing will happen between now and Saturday night to screw things up.

<u>Friday</u>

I told Uncle Gary about the dance, and he seems even more excited about it than I am. He wanted to know all the details, like how many people were gonna be there and if they hired a DJ. But I didn't know the answers to his questions, because Rowley's the one on the Dance Committee and that stuff is kind of in his department.

I was more focused on finding something to WEAR. Uncle Gary told me if I really want to impress my date, I should wear a suit. I went in Rodrick's closet and found a suit that he actually wore to one of Uncle Gary's weddings.

I couldn't find any cologne in Rodrick's junk drawer, but I DID find a bottle of that body spray they're always advertising on TV. I was a little nervous about using it, though, because if that stuff really works like they say in the ads, then tomorrow night could be a nightmare.

My Great Uncle Bruce passed away a few years ago, and I knew we had a box with some of his personal stuff in the garage. I found a bottle of his cologne and tried a little on my wrist.

It made me smell exactly like Great Uncle Bruce, but I figure it's safer than using that body spray.

168

I even asked Dad to take me to the grocery store, where I bought a box of those Valentine's chocolates for Abigail. I never should've taken the cellophane off the box, though, because I've already helped myself to the buttercreams, peanut clusters, and caramels.

Hopefully, Abigail likes the coconut chocolates and the ones that taste like toothpaste, because that's all that's really left at this point.

Saturday
Tonight was the night of the big Valentine's Day dance, and it got off to a REALLY rough start.

When I went over to Rowley's house to get ready, I noticed he had little red bumps on his face that looked like mosquito bites. But then I realized what those spots were: CHICKEN POX.

Ever since Evan Whitehead showed up at school with chicken pox a few weeks ago, it's been spreading like wildfire in my class.

This past week four boys were sent home by the school nurse. I'm pretty sure one of those guys was the Mad Pantser, because there haven't been any pantsing incidents since Tuesday.

I've heard chicken pox are SUPER contagious, and whenever a kid gets them, they're not allowed to come back to school for a week. But I couldn't afford to have Rowley out of commission for even one NIGHT. He was my ride to the dance, and I knew that if his mom and dad didn't let him go, then I couldn't go, either.

I told Rowley he had the chicken pox, but I probably should've broken the news to him slowly instead of all at once.

Rowley was gonna go straight downstairs and tell his parents, but I told him to calm down and we'd figure this out together.

I said if he could just get through the night without telling anyone, I'd owe him for the rest of my life. All he needed to do was cover up his chicken pox and not make a big stink to his parents. We'd both go to the dance and have a great time, and no one would even have to know.

But Rowley was too freaked out to think straight, and I had to give him two coconut chocolates to quiet him down.

Now that Rowley knew he had the chicken pox, he was going CRAZY with the itching. So I got some socks out of his dresser and put them on his hands.

I figured Rowley's mom and dad probably knew what chicken pox looked like and we had to find a way to cover them up. So we went into his parents' bathroom and looked through his Mom's makeup kit to see if there was anything we could use. I found some stuff called "concealer," and that sounded about right to me.

I used a little brush I found in a drawer and then tried to cover up the problem areas on Rowley's face.

But you could totally tell that Rowley was wearing makeup. So I grabbed a silk scarf from the top of Mrs. Jefferson's dresser and told Rowley to put it on and cover up around his mouth. Then I noticed he had a few chicken pox on his FOREHEAD, so I found a beach hat in his mom's closet and had him put that on, too.

173

I'm not gonna say Rowley looked totally normal, but at least you couldn't tell he had the chicken pox.

I kind of held my breath when we got into the car, but I think Mr. Jefferson just thought Rowley's getup was some kind of middle school fashion thing, and he didn't say a word.

When I opened the back door to get in, I was pretty surprised to find Rowley's old booster seat taking up one of the spots.

I asked Rowley why he still had a booster seat in his dad's car, and he said they just never took it out once he got big enough for the regular seat. But come to think of it, I've always thought Rowley seemed a little too tall whenever he drove by with his family.

I knew we had to take that thing out before we went to pick up Abigail, because a limo company would never have a booster seat in one of its cars.

But you needed to be some kind of an engineer to figure out how to undo the clasp on that thing. By that point we were already late picking up Abigail, so we had to just leave it.

When we pulled into Abigail's driveway, I asked Mr. Jefferson to honk the horn to let her know we were there.

But Mr. Jefferson wouldn't honk the horn, because he said that's no way to treat a "lady." He said one of us was gonna have to go to her front door and "escort" her.

Rowley started to get out, but I realized this was my big chance to make a good first impression on Abigail. So I walked up to the house and knocked on the door.

But Abigail didn't come to the front door
— her DAD did. Apparently, Mr. Brown is
a state trooper, or he just likes dressing up
like one.

Mr. Brown said Abigail was upstairs getting
ready and she'd be down in a minute.

He told me to come inside and have a seat while I waited. It felt like we were sitting there an HOUR waiting for Abigail to come downstairs, and I really didn't like the look of the handcuffs Mr. Brown had on his belt.

I finally decided this was way too much stress for a Valentine's Day dance and was ready to bail out. But right as I went to leave, Abigail came down the stairs.

The first thing I noticed was that Abigail was wearing a really poofy dress, and I knew there was no way the three of us were gonna fit in the backseat of Mr. Jefferson's car. But there was no way I was sitting in Rowley's booster seat, either, so I volunteered to ride up front. Besides, I knew Mr. Jefferson had heated front seats, so I figured I might as well take advantage of that.

Mr. Jefferson had a pile of papers in the passenger seat because I guess he was planning on doing his taxes or something while he was waiting for us at the dance.

It was too much of a hassle to move all that stuff, so I decided to just hop in the way back of the car so we could get on with the night.

Abigail didn't seem too bothered by the fact that Rowley was sitting in a booster seat, and I'm pretty sure she thought he was just doing it as a joke.

But humor is kind of MY thing, and I wasn't about to let Rowley steal my thunder.

It got kind of quiet in the car, so I asked Mr. Jefferson if he could turn on the radio. But instead of putting on some music, he tuned in to some boring talk radio station, and that's what we had to listen to for the rest of the ride.

I'm pretty sure he just did that because he was annoyed I'd called him "Driver."

Rowley and Abigail got into a conversation, but I was right next to the speakers in the back and I couldn't really hear what they were saying.

When Mr. Jefferson pulled over, I thought
we were at the restaurant. But we'd stopped
at a repair shop to pick up Mr. Jefferson's
vacuum cleaner.

At that point I wished I'd just coughed
up the money for a limo, because a
professional driver wouldn't have run
errands on the way to the restaurant.

I'd made a reservation at Spriggo's, which
is that fancy restaurant Mom and Dad are
always talking about. I knew it might be a
little pricey, but I'd saved up a lot of money
from chores and I really wanted to impress
Abigail by looking like a big shot.

When we pulled into the parking lot, Mr.
Jefferson opened the back for me. But when
I got out, my suit was covered in all these
greasy smears from the vacuum cleaner.

I didn't want to look like a slob, so I just left
my jacket in the car, and we went into the
restaurant together. I was hoping Rowley
would take a hint and stay back with his
dad, but he came right along with us.

Spriggo's was a LOT fancier than I thought it would be. When we walked in, the host told us this was an "upscale establishment" and that gentlemen were required to wear sports jackets.

But there was no way I was gonna wear my dirty suit jacket, so I asked the host if he could just make an exception this one time. He said he couldn't but that the restaurant had spare sports jackets I could borrow. The one he gave me was a little big, but I put it on anyway.

When we sat down I noticed a terrible smell and tried to figure out where it was coming from. Then I realized it was coming from ME. I guess that loaner jacket had been used by a hundred different people without ever being washed.

I didn't want to smell like somebody else's body odor during dinner, so I excused myself to go to the bathroom and scrubbed the sports jacket's underarms with soap and water, then dried them with the hand dryer.

Well, that just made it WORSE, because the heat activated the B.O. and it spread.

That was it for me. I told Abigail and Rowley this place was for phonies and we should just take off.

I left my jacket with the host at the front, and the three of us walked out the door. I said maybe we should just skip dinner and go right to the dance, but Abigail said she was really hungry, and Rowley said HE was starving, too.

The only other restaurant in the area was Corny's, and I told them there was no way I was going THERE. But Rowley said he really likes the dessert bar at Corny's, and Abigail said that sounded good to her.

I was really starting to regret having Rowley along on this date, because if all he was gonna do was take Abigail's side, I'd get outvoted every single time. But I didn't want to make a big deal about it in the middle of my date, so I just bit my lip and we walked three blocks to Corny's.

Luckily, I remembered about the tie issue before we walked in the front door, and I stuffed mine in my back pocket at the last second.

But I didn't have time to warn Rowley, so now his tie is a permanent part of the Wall of Shame.

Corny's was a total ZOO. My family usually goes on a weeknight, but it's a whole different scene on a Saturday.

The good news was that since we didn't have any little kids with us, they didn't seat us in Children's Alley. But the "adult" section of Corny's wasn't a whole lot better. All that separates the two sides is some glass, and we got seated right next to a family with a bunch of wild kids.

I asked our waitress if we could move, and she made a sour face and took our stuff to another table. But I wish we had just stayed where we were, because our new situation wasn't an improvement.

I didn't want to ask the waitress to move us a SECOND time, because the last person you want to make mad is the person who's serving you your food. So I put a couple of menus up against the window to block my view.

Our waitress brought us corn chips, and Rowley took the socks off his hands so he could eat. I didn't think it was such a great idea for all of us to be grabbing chips out of the same basket while Rowley had the chicken pox, so I kept it near me.

Every time Rowley looked like he wanted a chip, I pushed one to him with a straw.

SLIDE

I couldn't remember if the chicken pox is airborne, so whenever Rowley talked I held my breath just to be sure.

At one point he told us a really long story about something that happened to him last summer, and by the end I almost passed out.

I told Abigail and Rowley that I was paying for dinner so they should get whatever they wanted. I was trying to show off a little for Abigail by throwing my money around.

But when the waitress came back, Abigail ordered TWO appetizers, and so did Rowley.

The waitress couldn't understand what Rowley was saying because of his scarf, though, and he pulled it down to speak. But when he did, a single molecule of spit flew in the air and landed on my bottom lip.

I let my jaw go totally slack so the molecule wouldn't get into my mouth. I tried to stay calm on the outside, but on the inside I was totally freaking out.

I wanted to wipe my lip with my napkin, but I'd dropped it on the floor and couldn't reach it. So I waited until Abigail was distracted and then wiped my lip on her sleeve.

We placed our order, and I asked for a plain hamburger to save money. Abigail ordered the T-bone steak, which is the most expensive item on the menu, and Rowley got the same thing even though I was trying to signal for him to order something cheap.

When our food came out, my hamburger had lettuce and tomato on it, because at Corny's they ALWAYS get your order wrong. I took off the lettuce and tomato, but there was mayonnaise on my burger, too.

When our waitress came around again, I told her I'd ordered a burger with nothing on it. So she took a napkin and just wiped the mayonnaise off, then left the napkin right in the middle of the table.

I lost my appetite after that. But even if I WAS hungry, I probably wouldn't have finished my meal anyway. If you clean your plate at Corny's, there's a picture at the bottom that I really can't stand.

I just sat there and waited while Abigail and Rowley ate their steaks, and when they finished I signaled for the waitress to come over so I could pay the bill.

But then Rowley and Abigail said they wanted dessert. The whole reason we came to Corny's in the first place was for the dessert bar, which comes free with your meal. But of course Rowley and Abigail each wanted to order a SPECIAL dessert off the menu, which costs extra.

I got up and found our waitress to tell her it was Rowley's birthday, because I knew then he'd get a free dessert. So a few minutes later the waiters and waitresses all came out and sang "Happy Birthday" to Rowley and gave him his free cake.

Abigail still ordered a triple-layer chocolate cheesecake, which she only took two bites out of.

When the bill came, I couldn't BELIEVE how much it was. I had to use all the money in my wallet, and I even had to pull out the five dollars I was keeping in my sock in case of an emergency.

196

The waitress wouldn't take the money I
had in my sock because it was a little wet,
so I had to go out to the car and ask Mr.
Jefferson if he had a five-dollar bill he could
trade.

When I got back to the table, Rowley
and Abigail were in the middle of a
conversation, and it seemed to me like they
were sitting a little closer than when I'd left.

I thought about giving Abigail a heads-up that she might want to keep her distance from Rowley, but I was afraid she'd bail on the date if she found out about the chicken pox.

The three of us got back in the car, and Mr. Jefferson drove us to school and dropped us off at the front door. He gave Rowley a big hug, which I'm sure seemed pretty weird to Abigail if she thought he really was a professional driver.

HAVE A WONDERFUL TIME!

HUG

?

The theme of the dance was "Midnight in Paris," and I have to admit the Dance Committee did a pretty good job. The gym was decked out to look like a street in France. There was a long table set up with punch and snacks, and there was even a chocolate fountain with strawberries for dipping.

We handed over our tickets and then got in line for photos. Each couple had their picture taken in front of a backdrop of Paris.

When it was our turn, I stood with Abigail and the photographer snapped our photo. But I wish I'd known Rowley was gonna get in the picture WITH us, because I would've just skipped it.

Midnight in Paris
Valentine's Dance

Something about the DJ looked familiar to me, and when I got closer I realized it was Uncle Gary. Don't even ask me how HE got the job.

Uncle Gary must've seen it as an opportunity to unload his T-shirts on my classmates. It was dark in the gym, so kids didn't know they were getting ripped off.

One minute Abigail was standing right next to me, and the next she was gone. I finally spotted her on the other side of the gym talking with her friends.

I walked over to them, but before I got there they all went into the girls' bathroom together.

I have no idea what it is about girls that makes them go to the bathroom in groups, but something about it happening NOW really made me nervous.

I didn't know what Abigail thought of me, but I figured she was probably telling her friends right at that moment. The boys' bathroom is right next to the girls' in the gym, so I went in there and pressed my ear to the wall.

I could hear a lot of giggling, but I couldn't really make out the conversation because of all the racket in the boys' bathroom.

I tried to get people to stop making noise, but it was no use.

It got quiet on the other side of the wall, so I walked back into the gym, and Abigail and her friends were over by the punch.

At 7:50, Uncle Gary turned up the music, and it looked like the dance was gonna get started for real. But that's when some people my Gramma's age started trickling in.

By 8:00 there must have been a hundred of them crowded around the entrance. There was some sort of commotion between one of the teachers and a few of the senior citizens, so I got closer to see what was going on.

The senior citizens claimed they'd booked the gym for a town meeting about the new Senior Center. Mrs. Sheer told them she reserved the gym for the dance two weeks ago.

But the seniors said they reserved it two MONTHS ago, and they had the paperwork to prove it. The Senior Center people said us kids were gonna have to clear out of the gym so they could have their meeting.

But then some of the girls on the Dance
Committee got in on the conversation, and
it looked like it was about to get ugly.

Just when it seemed like a fight was gonna
break out, Mrs. Sheer suggested a
compromise. She said we could put up the
partition in the middle of the gym and the
seniors could have their meeting on one
half and us kids could have our dance on
the other.

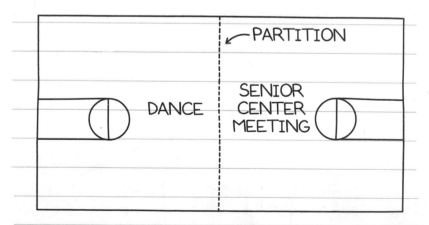

Everybody seemed to be able to live with that idea, and the janitor put up the partition.

Losing half of the gym was kind of a bummer, but what killed the mood was the LIGHTS. There's only one switch for the overhead lights in the gym, and they had to be either all on or all off. The senior citizens wanted them on for their meeting, so that was the end of the "Midnight in Paris" vibe over on our side of the gym.

The bright lights were bad for Uncle Gary, too, because now all the kids who bought shirts from him could see they'd gotten ripped off, and they started demanding their money back.

Uncle Gary tried to distract everyone by turning the music up, and a lot of people hit the dance floor.

The girls danced in a big group in the middle of the gym. Every once in a while a guy would try to dance his way into the group, but the girls had formed a kind of wall that kept the boys out. I didn't really understand that until I tried to make a move to break into the circle and got totally blocked.

One of the seniors came over to our side of the gym and complained that the music was too loud and it needed to be turned way down.

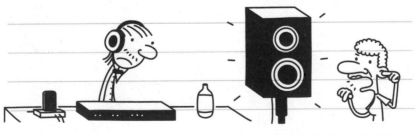

So Uncle Gary lowered the volume by about 80%, and then we could hear every word of the Senior Center meeting.

LET THE RECORD SHOW THAT MRS. FISHBURN HAS SECONDED THE MOTION TO HAVE A COFFEEMAKER IN THE KITCHENETTE.

That didn't seem to bother the girls, though. A lot of them took out their personal music players and just kept dancing.

By that point most of the boys had had enough. All that time being on their best behavior around the girls had taken its toll, and a lot of the guys just totally cut loose.

Mrs. Sheer and the rest of the chaperones tried to calm the boys down, but it was hopeless. It was a really wild scene, and it was actually getting a little dangerous.

I thought about going over by the bleachers to get out of everyone's way, but at that moment the Mad Pantser struck again and I decided I was better off where I was.

Every once in a while, a few latecomers would walk in and turn right back around when they saw what was happening in the gym. But at around 9:00, Michael Sampson walked in holding hands with Cherie Bellanger.

Michael was the boy Abigail was SUPPOSED to go to the dance with, but I guess his "family obligation" story was just a lie.

And judging from the look on his face, I don't think he was expecting Abigail to be there, either.

After that, it was just a whole lot of drama. Michael took off and left his date behind, and Abigail spent the next half hour bawling her eyes out in the corner of the gym.

I did what I could to help make Abigail feel better, but she kind of had a crowd around her, so I'm not sure she actually noticed.

212

Right about that time, the Senior Center meeting wrapped up, and a few of the seniors started drifting over to our side of the gym and helping themselves to the refreshments.

They went through the strawberries pretty quick, and then there was nothing for people to dip in the chocolate fountain.

So kids started sticking their fingers directly in the fountain, and it was Corny's all over again.

One kid lost a contact lens in the chocolate fountain, and Mrs. Sheer had everyone stand back so she could fish it out when it cycled back through.

Since the meeting was over, Uncle Gary turned the music back up.

214

But the old folks started making song requests, and the next thing you knew, our Valentine's Day dance was overrun by senior citizens.

I just watched everything play out from my spot against the back wall, wondering why I'd even wanted to go to the dance in the first place. I was also starting to regret not wearing the body spray I found in Rodrick's junk drawer, because Great Uncle Bruce's cologne was attracting people outside my age group.

It was almost 10:00, and Uncle Gary announced that the next song would be the last one of the night. When the music started playing, a few kids paired up and walked out on the dance floor as couples, which was the first time that had happened all night.

I couldn't wait for the song to end, because this dance was a total disaster, and I just wanted to go home and play some video games so I could erase the whole experience from my brain.

But just when I thought things couldn't get any worse, I saw Ruby Bird and she was coming right for me.

216

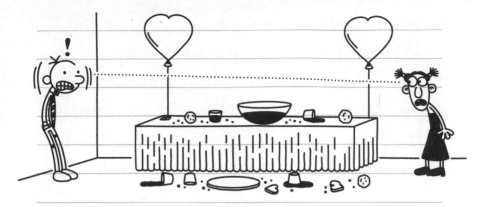

I didn't know if she was gonna ask me to dance or if I'd somehow done something to make her mad, but I did not want to end up getting bitten at a middle school dance.

I looked for some way to escape, but I was trapped. Luckily, Abigail walked right out of the bathroom at that exact moment, and I grabbed her hand just before Ruby got to me.

Abigail's makeup was a mess from all the crying, but I didn't really care. I was just happy to have an excuse to get away from Ruby. And to be honest with you, I think Abigail was happy to see me, too, so I led her to an empty spot on the dance floor.

I'd never slow-danced with a girl before, so I didn't know where I was supposed to put my hands. She put hers on my shoulders, and I put mine in my pockets, but that felt kind of dumb. So we met in the middle, and that seemed about right.

Then I noticed something on Abigail's chin. It was a little red bump that looked EXACTLY like one of Rowley's chicken pox.

Now, before I say what happened next, let me just explain in my defense that I was already on edge about the whole chicken pox thing.

But I admit, I MAY have overreacted a little.

It turns out it WASN'T chicken pox, though. It was just a pimple. When Abigail was crying, her makeup must've washed off her chin.

Anyway, I know that NOW, but anyone in my shoes probably would've reacted the same exact way I did.

But I don't think Abigail saw it that way, because on the ride home she wasn't real chatty with me.

When we pulled up to Abigail's house, Rowley walked her to the front door. That was fine with me, because it gave me a chance to finish off the rest of the chocolates. And after the night I just had, I was totally STARVING.

<u>Wednesday</u>

A lot has happened since the Valentine's Day dance.

A few days ago Uncle Gary bought a bunch of scratch tickets with the money he made selling T-shirts, and one of his tickets was a forty-thousand-dollar winner. So he paid Dad the money he owed him, wished me luck with the "ladies," and moved out of the house.

The other big news is that I got a full-blown case of the chicken pox.

I can't say for sure how I got them, but I really hope it wasn't from Rowley, because I'm not that crazy about the idea of a bunch of Rowley's virus cells attacking my immune system.

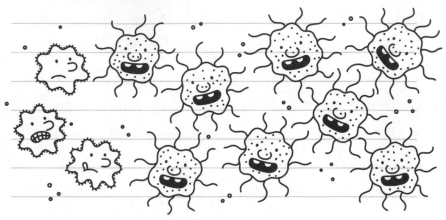

I'm pretty sure I DIDN'T get the chicken pox from Rowley, though. I've seen him walking to school the past few days, and from what I can tell, he's been wearing his mom's makeup on his chin. So I think those red bumps might've been pimples, just like Abigail's.

And speaking of Rowley and Abigail, I heard that the two of them are a couple now. All I can say is if that's true, it makes Rowley the worst wingman in history.

222

I'm supposed to stay home from school for at least a week. The good news is that with everyone out of the house, I can take long baths without anyone bothering me.

But I will admit all that floating around isn't as great as I remember it, and after just an hour your skin gets all wrinkly. So don't ask me how I lived that way for nine months.

Plus, I get a little lonely being by myself all day. Or at least I THINK I'm alone. Today I had a fresh towel next to the tub, and when I opened my eyes it was gone.

So either somebody's messing with me, or Johnny Cheddar is at it again.

ACKNOWLEDGMENTS

Thanks to my wonderful family for all your encouragement and for all the laughs. A lot of our stories are laced in these books, and it's been great fun to share this adventure with all of you.

Thanks to everyone at Abrams for publishing these books and for putting so much care into making them as good as they can be. Thanks to Charlie Kochman for treating every book like it's the first. Thanks to Michael Jacobs for everything you've done to make Greg Heffley reach his full potential. Thanks to Jason Wells, Veronica Wasserman, Scott Auerbach, Chad W. Beckerman, and Susan Van Metre for your dedication and for your fellowship. We've had lots of good times, and there are many more to come.

Thanks to everyone at my job — Jess Brallier and the entire team at Poptropica — for your support, camaraderie, and dedication to creating great stories for kids.

Thanks to Sylvie Rabineau, my terrific agent, for your encouragement and guidance. Thanks to Elizabeth Gabler, Carla

Hacken, Nick D'Angelo, Nina Jacobson, Brad Simpson, and David Bowers for bringing Greg Heffley and his family to life on the big screen.

Thanks to Shaelyn Germain for making things run smoothly behind the scenes and for helping in so many ways.

226

ABOUT THE AUTHOR

Jeff Kinney is a #1 *New York Times* bestselling author and a six-time Nickelodeon Kids' Choice Award winner for Favorite Book. Jeff has been named one of *Time* magazine's 100 Most Influential People in the World. He is also the creator of Poptropica, which was named one of *Time* magazine's 50 Best Websites. He spent his childhood in the Washington, D.C., area and moved to New England in 1995. Jeff lives with his wife and two sons in Massachusetts, where they own a bookstore, An Unlikely Story.

The employees of Thorndike Press hope you have enjoyed this Large Print book. All our Thorndike, Wheeler, and Kennebec Large Print titles are designed for easy reading, and all our books are made to last. Other Thorndike Press Large Print books are available at your library, through selected bookstores, or directly from us.

For information about titles, please call:
  (800) 223-1244

or visit our Web site at:
  http://gale.cengage.com/thorndike

To share your comments, please write:
  Publisher
  Thorndike Press
  10 Water St., Suite 310
  Waterville, ME 04901